SEVEN LI

SEVEN LIVES

almost everything can be taken from an individual
but his or her story

vladimir azarov

EXILE
editions

Library and Archives Canada Cataloguing in Publication

Azarov, Vladimir, 1935-, author
    Seven lives : almost everything can be taken from an individual but his or her
story / Vladimir Azarov.

Poems.
Issued in print and electronic formats.
ISBN 978-1-55096-391-5 (pbk.).--ISBN 978-1-55096-392-2 (pdf)

    I. Title.
PS8601.Z37S49 2014   C811'.6   C2014-900188-6
                                          C2014-900189-4

Copyright © Vladimir Azarov, 2014
Preface copyright © Ewan Whyte, 2014
Drawings copyright © Deborah Barnett, 2014
Cover Image copyright © Ilia Efimovich Repin (1844–1930); The Volga Boatmen
(1870–1873). Used by permission of the State Russian Museum, St. Petersburg.

Design and Composition by Mishi Uroboros
Typeset in Bembo font at Moons of Jupiter Studios

Published by Exile Editions Ltd ~ www.ExileEditions.com
144483 Southgate Road 14 — GD, Holstein, Ontario, N0G 2A0
Printed and Bound in Canada in 2014, by Imprimerie Gauvin

We gratefully acknowledge, for their support toward our publishing activities, the Canada
Council for the Arts, the Government of Canada through the Canada Book Fund (CBF),
the Ontario Arts Council, and the Ontario Media Development Corporation.

Canadian Sales: The Canadian Manda Group, 165 Dufferin Street,
Toronto ON M6K 3H6 www.mandagroup.com 416 516 0911

North American and International Distribution, and U.S. Sales:
Independent Publishers Group, 814 North Franklin Street,
Chicago IL 60610 www.ipgbook.com toll free: 1 800 888 4741

for my family

CONTENTS

PREFACE

Seven Lives is Vladimir Azarov's childhood experiences of Soviet life transformed into a poetic witnessing. into a poetic witnessing. Growing up in Kazakhstan, it was hidden from him that his family was in political exile. At the time, he thought "people must always be coming to these difficult Soviet work colonies in the east from all parts of the country." This gave him an unrealistic optimism which helped him to overcome many of the challenges of his life at the time and to find his own way to live in that artificial world.

"One must dare to be happy," says Azarov of this perceived blindness. He cannot remember who other than Gertrude Stein said this but it became his philosophy.

These poems, written in the form of short stories, are remarkable in their ability to bring past moments and lost times to life. Azarov does this with effortless ease. His ability to bring immediacy of experience and the poignancy of loss into the reader's current imagination in bittersweet poetic renderings often makes the listener or reader wait on the edge of his or her own imagination for the next turn of the story.

For me, it is his ability to find small moments of poetic arrest, like half-hidden flowers in scarified landscapes, which interrupt some of the bleak and desperate times he has lived through.

Making art from memory is not as easy to do as is commonly thought. There is a frequent tendency to underestimate the difficulty of this simple style that requires what Tolstoy called a "sincerity" of expression.

Azarov writes variations on famous works of literature, interweaving new possible readings and interpretations. But it is when he writes about the common sufferings of people he has known, often suffering from the intolerance and paranoia of the Soviet regime, that he is at his best. In his poem "Rag Doll" where his feeling for the captured and very skinny German soldier, who was unnecessarily beaten up by the poet's father while the family was in exile in Kazakhstan in 1945, is still a vibrant memory. It is as though Azarov has made friends with exile and he is able to relate to his sorrow as a kind of comfort.

These events and times that seem so remote are not so remote, and their terrifying import could easily be recycled in our future history. In this, though, there will always be bursts of laughter, and the enjoyment of art will always be there as a possible salve for the absurd sufferings we inflict on each other in history.

—EWAN WHYTE

One must dare to be happy.

—GERTRUDE STEIN

OVERTURE

THE SONG OF THE VOLGA BOATMEN

(Russian Folk Song)

Yo, heave ho!
Yo, heave ho!
Once more, once again, still once more

Yo, heave ho!
Yo, heave ho!
Once more, once again, still once more

Now we fell the stout birch tree,
Now we pull hard: one, two, three.
Ay-da, da, ay-da!
Ay-da, da, ay-da!
Now we pull hard: one, two, three.
Now we pull hard: one, two, three.

Yo, heave ho!
Yo, heave ho!
Once more, once again, still once more

As the barges float along,
To the sun we sing our song.
Ay-da, da, ay-da!
Ay-da, da, ay-da!
To the sun we sing our song.

Hey, hey, let's heave along the way
To the sun we sing our song

Yo, heave ho!
Yo, heave ho!
Once more, once again, still once more

Oh, you, Volga, mother river,
Mighty stream so deep and wide.
Ay-da, da, ay-da!
Ay-da, da, ay-da!
Volga, Volga, mother river.

Yo, heave ho!
Yo, heave ho!
Once more, once again, still once more

Yo, heave ho!
Yo, heave ho!

TO AUNT SHURA

PART ONE

RED ARMY MEN'S CHORUS:
>   Yo, heave ho!
>   yo, heave ho!
> once more, once again, still once more—
> trees shake and the grass bows down
> obedient to the blowing wind—
> we pull hard: one, two, three,
> to tell the story, witness to the past—
> Aunt Shura's story:
>   ay-da, da, ay-da!
>   ay-da, da, ay-da!

MYSELF TO MYSELF:
> Aunt Shura is my last aunt in Moscow
> and she is also Aunt Sasha or Alexandra or
> Andrevna (her patronymic—
> Andrey is my grandfather).
> I hadn't seen her for more than a decade and I'd
> almost forgotten how she looks and her voice—
> her bird-like squeak,
> her small-town-near-Moscow talk,
> the town of Tula,
> the hard Russian "r" and
> her smooth long
> Moscow "a"—like a song taking its time
> as she hurries toward me, still
> erect, still confident in her step!
> She sounds like she sings:

AUNT SHURA:

"O-o-oh my loving ne-e-ephew!
You come to me bearing our
family's old name.
My true relative, my living blood.
At last I see you, dear child.
Let me hug you."

MYSELF TO MYSELF:

I had not seen her for more than a decade:
a salad on the white tablecloth
herring oiled and onioned, a hot potato
thinly sliced, smoked pork sausage,
no caviar, not on
my aunt's pension.
We are sitting around the table—
her granddaughter,
a middle-aged computer woman,
me, her nephew, the biblical "Prodigal Son,"
and
an aunt's great-granddaughter,
a Moscow Juniors champion
in the SHOT PUT, which is, for me,
huge news.

RED ARMY MEN'S CHOIR:
> Yo, heave ho!
>
> yo, heave ho!

once more, once again, still once more,
now we pull hard: one, two, three—
a young female in the middle of a
military family—
(the aunt's husband and her son both were
Russian warriors).

AUNT SHURA:
"To our unexpected long-expected meeting!"

RED ARMY MEN'S CHORUS:
> Yo, heave ho!
>
> yo, heave ho!

once more, once again, still once more—
Russian birches, oaks, firs!
wormwood and feather-grass.
Aunt Shura clinks her vodka's crystal shot glass.
She's 93.

PART TWO

AUNT SHURA:

Metal shavings swirl in the
plant's heavy air.
My unprotected hands hold
a shining metal detail.
I am a happy girl of 30
a small but important screw
in the cogs of industry.
I am working a machine
in a plant in the city of Tula,
cradle of the Russian military.
We must save our young country.

RED ARMY MEN'S CHORUS:

Yo, heave ho!
yo, heave ho!
once more, once again, still once more,
now we pull hard: one, two, three!
ay-da, da, ay-da!
ay-da, da, ay-da!

AUNT SHURA:

So many voracious enemies.
Imperialists! Capitalists! Fascists!
Our plant's Comrade Party Leader said:
"We live in the industrial epoch."
Now industry is my passion although

I am a girl!

I knew a name, Demidov.

He lived in Tula back in the 18th century.

The same idea.

INDUSTRIALIZATION!

Hey, nephew!

Remember? This Russian name? You,

my apolitical paper-shuffling little artist.

Three hundred years ago a talented Tulan smithy,

Nikita Demidov, was

visited by Great Peter

who said: "Hey! Tulan Smithy.

See this, my Dutch gun? Make me the same.

But not right now. Tomorrow. And

I will come for this new Russian gun."

I'd always liked this Demidov story, about the

beginning of Russia's weapons superiority.

PART THREE

RED ARMY MEN'S CHOIR:

    Yo, heave ho!

    yo, heave ho!

once more, once again, still once more.

"We cannot make a revolution

wearing silk gloves." Who says?

Ah-h-h, forget it. Remember—Stalin.

Now we pull hard: one, two, three

    ay-da, da, ay-da!

    ay-da, da, ay-da!

AUNT SHURA:

Metal shavings swirl in the heavy air.

I remember our leader's words:

I was working without gloves

in a row of young Soviet girls!

Free girls. Freedom. Freedom, I made it myself.

I ran off from my unhappy home.

I hope you, my nephew, know our family history:

Grandpa in hiding, fearing arrest

because he'd become rich through hard work

before the Revolution, being

the builder of several Moscow landmarks

including the Hotel Metropol

near Red Square, raised by

his hand, his brain. Not its great

mosaic or ceramic façade,

but the walls, the roof.
Grandfather's triumph,
Remember—
I just saw, in passing, his (our) two expropriated
Moscow houses equipped at the end
of the 19th century with a talking Ericsson,
like Lenin's cabinet.

PART FOUR

RED ARMY MEN'S CHORUS:
> Yo, heave ho!
> yo, heave ho!
once more, once again, still once more.
Oh Volga, Volga, our pride.
Of the Volga River and the sun we sing
but our air reeks of WWII.
> Ay-da, da, ay-da!
> Ay-da, da, ay-da!

AUNT SHURA:
Metal shavings swirl in the heavy air
and unexpectedly
he stopped me,
a military student,
my future pilot, Alex.
"Stop playing the blonde manly fool,"
he told me.
"You are a girl, a future woman.
Mother of my future children."
He, my Alex,
shivers from a slight fever
in a hospital for Red military pilots.

RED ARMY MEN'S CHORUS:

>Yo, heave ho!
>
>Yo, heave ho!
>
>Ay-da, da, ay-da!
>
>Ay-da, da, ay-da!

AUNT SHURA:

But still no WWII.

Alex lies down, he can't walk.

The Red Army's flying soldier

is ill, his temperature high.

The end of June, the day is Sunday,

the Red-starred soldier-nurse brings

shots of vodka to the ward.

The roar of airplanes.

Still peaceful military craft but

a constant noise around the airfield,

above the hospital for pilots.

Still, it is not WWII.

Alex lay down, he couldn't walk.

PART FIVE

MYSELF TO MYSELF:
  I admire my aunt's energy.
  She wipes her dry eyes,
  she is 93,
  she smiles.
  June of '41
  is quite clear in her memory.
  She remembers it
  like yesterday, that sunny Sunday
  without Alex,
  yet close enough to her in the military hospital
  near Moscow!

AUNT SHURA:
  "Guys. Bad news. Hey, listen!"

RED ARMY MEN'S CHOIR:
      Yo, heave ho!
      yo, heave ho!
  once more, once again, still once more—
  Oh, despite the loud noise of
  military planes
  we hear your voice, oh mother,
  and Father Stalin's voice:
  "The whole Soviet people must fight for
  every inch of Soviet soil."
  We pull hard: one, two, three,

ay-da, da, ay-da!
ay-da, da, ay-da!

MYSELF TO MYSELF:

My aunt cries along with the Red Army
military chorus,
vodka glass in hand.

AUNT SHURA:

"War! War! War with the Germans!
A Real War! Hitler invaded our country.
Hitler, who'd signed a Pact for Peace with us!"

MYSELF TO MYSELF:

My auntie settles in like she's
a real movie actress.
She sees Alex circling in his plane through
dark streaming clouds.

AUNT SHURA:

No longer bedridden during the war, he is
Alex in the sky in his cockpit.
He nibbles on aspirin along with his pilot's
portion of sweet-bitter chocolate.
June 26th,
four days of war,
his plane badly shot up,
his ship diving in flames
he crash-lands on its aluminum belly

in the tall grasses of Ukraine,
captured German territory.
What'll he do? My poor Alex.

RED ARMY MEN'S CHOIR:
      Yo, heave ho!
      yo, heave ho!
once more, once again, still once more.
"One death is a tragedy,
a million is a statistic," Stalin says.
Alex! you are one in a million.
The fires of war blaze above the earth.
We pull hard: one, two, three,
      ay–da, da, ay–da!
      ay–da, da, ay–da!

AUNT SHURA:
HE-E-EY! SO-O-OLDIER!
THE LAST CARTRIDGE IS YO-O-OURS!
Alex has heard Great Stalin's
merciless order:
"Die! No prisoners!"

PART SIX

AUNT SHURA:

Yes,

my Alex has a bullet for himself,

but he wants to stay alive to fight the war,

to raise our banner over Berlin!

He lunges into the forest

blasts of war echo

in his ears.

Where are the Germans? And where are our troops?

He meets a Ukrainian,

exchanges his khaki uniform and

becomes a local peasant dressed in an

embroidered blouse.

He is

near a Ukrainian village, no Germans to be seen,

but—

"There's a brave man in our national dress

but he's got a Soviet soldier's haircut."

He hears the voice of an unfriendly woman:

"Away! Hey! Away!

We won't die for you. Yet

we don't know who is better."

Alex takes off between the blue-white huts, darts

into the first open door that invites him in

to hide.

RED ARMY MEN'S CHOIR:
      Yo, heave ho!
      yo, heave ho!
once more, once again, still once more.
"This war is the war of the entire
Russian people," and
my Red Army pilot
meets a different woman
who takes hold of his hand to hide him
as all Soviet people during the War
do their duty.
Pull hard: one, two, three,
      ay-da, da, ay-da!
      ay-da, da, ay-da!

AUNT SHURA:
She leads him to the barn and
whispers, "Lie here between
these foul pigs.
Germans hate the stink
of Russian (Ukrainian: it's the same!) pigs."
A kind old woman brings hay and
spreads it on the damp earthen floor and covers
Alex with a blanket.

PART SEVEN

AUNT SHURA:

Hitler is dead! I cried that April day.
And now,
with Eva Braun and their dog
named Blonda—Oh! I remember—
but Alex was still flying
a couple of days after the May 9th victory,
conquering the last fascist stronghold,
flying over a trapped city,
Budapest. And then we had real Victory!
Real Peace!
Stillness. No vibrating cannonades
above my Alex's head,
but never friendly, never warm,
not quiet: only a
cold, sub-zero temperature.
Alex taking his family, i.e. me,
to Germany,
to the Russian Zone,
the isolation of foreign life,
no French/American contacts
behind the Soviet Iron Curtain.
I live like all members of
Russian military families.
I stand in line for food
and hear
the hissing whisper from some German

frau, "Die Russisch Schwein—sh-h-h,"
and listening, I smile.

RED ARMY MEN'S CHOIR:
       Yo, heave ho!
       yo, heave ho!
once more, once again, still once more.
German ladies! We Red Army men are
still marching
through your country!
As if you didn't know it,
the pigs belong to
Aunt Shura and Alex's friends.
The Russian swine have rescued Alex.
       Ay-da, da, ay-da!
       Ay-da, da, ay-da!

AUNT SHURA:
Whispering: "S-s-stalingr-r-rad."
Silence in the grocery.
I buy a kilo of a delicious German
porkwurst.

PART EIGHT

AUNT SHURA:

> "Oh dear nephew.
> You cannot eat Moscow
> pork sausage for fear of your heart.
> At my age, 93,
> long talk, long talk.
> Maybe I will inspire you,
> my nephew,
> to write poetry
> about our Army men, our Russian women
> who were with them?
> Here's to our unexpected
> and
> long expected meeting!"

RED ARMY MEN'S CHORUS:

> Yo, heave ho!
> yo, heave ho!
> once more, once again, still once more—
> Oh Volga, Volga! Our Pride!
> To the sun over the Volga
> we sing the song,
> to the fire blazing above the earth,
> to those Russian hogs who rescued Alex,
> to the trees blowing and grasses bowing,
> obedient to the Volga winds,

to an aunt clinking her crystal vodka
shot glass,
to her being 93!
     ay-da, da, ay-da!
     ay-da, da, ay-da!
     yo, heave ho!
     yo, heave ho!
once more, once again, still once more.

PART NINE

RED ARMY MEN'S CHORUS:
>   Yo, heave ho!
>   yo, heave ho!
once more, once again, still once more—
trees blowing and grasses bowing down.
Vladimir wants to tell his own story
before flying out to his new home
across an ocean,
the story of his other aunt, Valentina,
who came to Leningrad to nurse him
when he was born.
Aunt Valya—
Andreevna as a patronymic, just like Aunt Shura.
She was a villager.
She's no longer alive, died recently,
all tribute and peace to her.
Let's listen to all the people at the table
and to Aunt Shura
who is 93,
>   ay-da, da, ay-da!
>   ay-da, da, ay-da!
>   yo, heave ho!
>   yo, heave ho!
once more, once again, still once more.

Part Ten

MYSELF:
 I called my poem—

DUSK

The teal-blue dusk of August on
My grandparents' house bench in a Russian village

I am listening to a herd of cows coming in to sleep
In their home stalls after eating

Their day's fill in the meadows, before producing that indecent
Milk sound in the aluminum-silver pails in a

Dark space (I listened to it last night).
I am resting for a week after entering an arts

Institution. I am seventeen
I had forgotten the herdsman-god Hermes' plaster head

Which I had completed for an exam, a pencil
Line-drawing of Greek vases, conjugation with an ink

Mapping pen.
Village crickets chirp louder at night.

My Aunt Valentina comes and sits by me. She is a
Livestock doctor, a vet waiting for the cows,

Their heavy steps coming closer. Sometimes
A mooing sound.

"Oh! by the way!"—
My aunt mutters, "Your smart grandfather

Healed a dying cow! She'd eaten a poison weed. She lay
Absolutely still, just crying quietly and

Your grandfather cut the bottom off of a bottle and
Inserted the glass neck into the cow's anus to let loose

A power of wind." I wonder
If the herdsman I've sketched knows how to heal this way.

I wish
I knew more about the Greek god Hermes.

RED ARMY MEN'S CHORUS:
    Yo, heave ho!
    yo, heave ho!
once more, once again, still once more—
trees blowing and grasses bowing down.
Aunt Shura thanks Vladimir for his poem,
fey farewell kisses,

we all promise a repeat meeting.
Aunt Shura smiles, she's 93!
her girls behind her shift their feet

    ay-da, da, ay-da!

    ay-da, da, ay-da!

    yo, heave ho!

    yo, heave ho!

once more, once again, still once more.

LENINGRAD

LENINGRAD

Don't sleep, get up, you curly-haired girl!
Our country is on the rise toward fame!
—Soviet song by DMITRI SHOSTAKOVICH

Tam tram! Tam tram! Time runs on ahead.
Hold your head high. Tam tram. Tam. The future
Calls us on. Do not walk, run. Tram. On ahead.
On tam. On tram. On, on ahead.

St. Petersburg, Petrograd, Leningrad.
The evening. It is 6:30.
Fall. The fog-bound northern second city
Of the '30s—
A looming grey sky still at twilight
Shrouds the half-lit lamps. A tram throws off
A clammy warmth as it
Rumbles along the cobbled streetcar line.

The Nevsky is far behind. And the
Vasilevskyi will soon appear again.

A curly-haired girl
Leaves for home at the end of her day shift.
She's tired but
Cannot tear herself away from her loving entourage
Seen in the window, seen so many times.
A diminishing sky, dim electric lights

Dissolving the stucco window frames,
Lintels, columns, porches, and shop signs.
She sees a flashing movie poster.
City Lights again. Charlie Chaplin.
His sad laughter!

And *A Kiss from Mary Pickford*.
Mary's smiling face,
All the old movies,
Even this aghast, wailing woman
Is familiar to her.
Battleship Potemkin—
All screened so many times in the
City movie theatres.

She did not see *Potemkin,*
Although Lev Ivanovich,
Her friend at the Labour Club strongly suggested
She do so.
Then, she remembers that
She must pick up costumes from the Len-Film Studio
For a performance at the Labour Club of
The Three Muskateers. Yes, it will amuse
All the young workers.

A tram rumbles along the cobblestone road.
Tam tram. Tam tram.

A Shostakovich song
From a new movie, "Vstrechnyi," blasts through
The tram's open door

> *Don't sleep, get up, you curly-haired girl.*
> *Our country is on the rise toward fame.*

She crosses,
As she does every day,
The noisy Troitsky. The Bridge. The clack
Of metal banging
Against the metal segments of the bridge.
And she recalls:
This bridge is called Kirov now,
In memory of the leader who was
Murdered, yes, Kirov. She knows about this because of
Her club's new member. So enthusiastic, this fellow,
Hard working, a passionate scholar,
Brave, politically active,

And in her mind's eye, his kind smiling face.
A typical Leningrad fog-bound evening...
The dark cold waves of the Neva
Bring her back to reality:
Beautiful old Petersburg seen from the riverside,
The adored walls, the pediments, domes, spires...

That curly-haired girl? Maybe you've guessed, she's
My mother
Riding home after work.

But then, on another evening, another night,
She arrives at the Labourer Palace that is also
Her school.
She is running late.
Lev Ivanovich believes punctuality suggests a
Hard, diligent, preparation
For higher education.
Her dream is to become a qualified specialist...

She passes down the adult classes corridor:
"We are not slaves. Not slaves
Are we." The loud voices of the Workers
Faculty for Adult Students.
She's on the run.
Under Mayakovsky's slogan,
"Sail further into the Revolution"
On a bright red banner, down the long wall,
She runs
Hearing a soft voice that she knows. It calls:
"Hey, Curly! Hi!"
A bright smile is her answer.
He is in a hurry, too. She waves hello and tries
To run faster.

"Hey, stop! Hold on, Curly."
A tall fellow. Blond hair
Wet from wrestling at the sports club.
He is towelling sweat from his face.
"I haven't seen you for a while. Didn't you miss me?
Hey! Come on. Just a quick word."
(He is my father)
He's been to the club after a hot day of factory
Work where
Metal meets metal, where the hammer kisses the anvil,
Where he bends
Resistant iron wire into compliant rods,

And in the evening takes high-tech classes:
Proud to become a Soviet engineer,

Constructing
Future sonic-speed aircraft
To fly high. To the dialectical apex of Communism.
The proletariat's dream, to fly higher.
Higher.
He looks at his pocket watch—eight o'clock sharp.
Time for his class:

"See you later, Curly!"

The loudspeaker sings a jolly song:

Don't sleep, get up, you curly-haired girl.
Our country is on the rise toward fame.

She, the curly-haired girl, is not all smiles
At her workplace. Her head's bent
Over her work, her machines.
Now she is
No longer a girl,
Now she is married to the kind-hearted wrestler, my father.
But she is alone,
Her eyes blurred by tears because of the
Well-known Leningrad case of
Kirov's political murder…
The former curly-haired girl, a wife now,
Asks herself over
And over and over and over, but gets
No answer to her question:
Why was he arrested? Why? Such a huge mistake.
He is so honest, pure, innocent.
She feels she has to prepare for a dark future
With her newborn baby (yes, it is me)…

Another song:
Tangled iron rods.
Black forests of crooked iron trees.
Barbed wire twined all around them.
The bent crowd hauling themselves,

Having no Cross—this human ritual—
Perished. Only a merciless Red Sword
Hangs over their heads—bitter tears—
Stalin's steel repression…
But over the radio they're still singing
Even in the Gulag —

> Don't sleep, get up you, curly-haired girl.
> Our country is on the rise toward fame.

A COW NAMED
BEAUTY

A COW NAMED BEAUTY

for her good work
as an accountant at our
camp in
Kazakhstan my
mother

(who'd wanted when she was young
to be
a judge to pass judgement on
the enemies
of ordinary Soviets but

instead
had become
herself an exiled enemy)

she
got a generous bonus
as a gift – guess what?
ah-a-a!
nobody can guess.

A COW!

yes! a real domestic
cattle beast,
a real cow!

my mother came
home with
this news full of anxiety:
she'd never seen
live cows before
we'd come to
our new
settlement where twice
a day
the proud cows walked outside
as if they were
in New Delhi
but within a

couple of days
I stood beside my
mother and

together we saw
this
new member of our family.
my eyes were fixed on
her under stomach, her udder,
smooth round

breathing warmly

with her soft silk brown hair,
her tail, the cow swept

the evening's
insects away
and chewed her cud.
she
had a faraway look
in her eyes,

her deep dark sad
eyes, mournful
as an oriental thinker,
she looked so
submissive so peaceful

with her
small ivory horns curved
toward each other.

straight away
I loved this monster:

SHE IS A BEAUTY, I said.

she is named Beauty,
my mother told me.

my mother held
a thin green branch
but did not touch Beauty's
body, afraid

to insult her

baloony massive
Beauty who
shared the confines of our little barn
with two
white incubatored
chickens, the
inked
letters "A" (Azarov)
on their
brainless heads
and
rustling rats in
dark corners.

new life began:

now before going to school I had
a milky semolina
porridge

and my mom
had a
new friend.
Beauty smiled at Mother
every morning,
two female comrades

who parted for the day to do their
work until night—

the cow

her endless chewing
of Kazakh grass for our milk

my mother

clicking loudly on
an abacus, a bee
with an ariphmometer

every night my
mother
met Beauty with a bowl
and a wet wash
towel
for her udder

(as my mother said,
Beauty has girlishly modest
tits
with just enough milk for my porridge
and my mother's
coffee made from
acorns)

once when my
essay about Lenin's childhood
(I had written that
our genius liked
playing Beethoven's sonatas
with
his mother
Maria Alexandrovna)
was finished and

I waited
for the evening milk while
opening up *Uncle
Tom's Cabin*—
mother entered the room slowly
stepping

almost tragically

the empty bucket rang like
a church bell, alarmingly
but not too loud.

OUR
BEAUTY DOESN'T LIKE
US ANY MORE!

and continued

she gave a bit of milk
unwillingly
and then
kicked the bucket over
with her leg.
we have only
this poor glass of milk!

it is okay, I responded

listen, our teapot is hissing.

we will drink our tea.

and
I remembered
for the essay—that they had
played Schumann
& Schubert
four-handed!

and I wrote it down

time time time.
again,
our friend, our holy beast
called COW.
our Beauty. our
dear martyr

who lived humbly along with two
cackling chickens

and rustling rats.

who ended up eating
her prime beefsteaks?
some of the leaders of our special
settlement.

oh my Beauty!
your former
mistress master almost owner,
my mother,
she smiled at you

sometimes

remembering

your gentle temper
your wise sombre eyes
your comic little horns
your grudging milk

and also
my mother's
eternal touching of your—oh Beauty—
milkless udder—

my mother's
last amble with you
under the weeping
birches
of the Istra town cemetery
outside Moscow.

GREEN DROWNING

GREEN DROWNING

It must have been too cold for him, his heart gave way
—STEVIE SMITH. "Not waving but Drowning"

I

so many things
happened in our
settlement
during our special time—
our multicultural camp
Babylon.
I am a boy
of about 9, 10, 11,
in Kazakhstan during the end of
WWII.
I am in among the local
Kazakhs and Russian people
exiled by Stalin before the war
or moved from
Hitler's front
and also
there were the
Volga German children with their
Volga German mothers

II

so, this was the life
for all of us
with a little food
with German
movies
weekly in the barn
and with our very own lice,
those friends of war,
also
classes in school
with our teachers
and their "excellent" or "bad"
and the bullies.
the bullies.

III

and about those who were hurt,
of course I was among the latter,
and for what? I
was disciplined
(it was so disgusting.
I now oppose all such
practices), I was
suffering from a surplus of "excellent" marks.
even so, the
bullies like the non-bullies
all liked it when I told them
the *Count of Monte Cristo* story,
chapter by
chapter,
calling on my
perfect child's
memory
(now I sometimes forget
even my name—
sorry—
Vladimir?—
oh yes! thank you),
smooth talking
while at night
the school's electric lights
did not come on

IV

we had the river,
shallow but iced over for our
winter skates
made for us by adults
that led to
blood pouring from
my nose after
a bully pushed me
into the snow
and onto the ice.
it was Ha-a-ans,
my enemy
a stupid guy.
a Russian–German fascist.
I hated him.

V

once he beat me up on the way
home and
his German mother,
the cleaning woman in our
school,
probably a hard-working
peasant just
before the war who had
her strong roots,
her history in
Volga agriculture, dating back to
Catherine the Great,
and so she
ran to our barrack
to my mother,
who was tending to my painful
nose.
please DO NOT go to the
school board, he's my only
BABY.
I heard her German accent.
Hans? yes it was her Hans
her only BABY.
– baby? baby?
B-U-L-L-Y.
Hans,
soul-mate of all

bullies in the class,
Russians, Germans
even Kazakhs, all of them,
a flying swarm of bullies.

VI

And so this also passed,
days, weeks, semesters,
the early summer's
first heat under the
clouds
into early June
a free time with no classes
near my birthday
as
kids gravitated
to the water
and I also touched the
cold muddy river's face
with my
warm toes—
br-r-r! no, oh no.
it was still bathwater for me
but what is it?
unexpectedly
I hear a scream.
wild, scary.
AAAAAAAA!
he'd drowned! he was dead.
AAAAAAAA!
I saw
a boy's
skinny naked body.
it was green

VII

green green.
it's in my eyes now,
so clear,
tangled
muddy webs
hung
from his ears
across his face
his limbs
held by men who slipped and
slithered dangerously on
mucous
hummocks
along the bank as
they dragged the body
into the grass
onto dry land.
shivering I squeezed my
fists as
I stood nearby
feeling neither alive nor dead.

the crowd of children
was
enlarged by
crying women,
shuffling men.
I came to my senses.
I was afraid to recognize
him—whom?
HIM
yes. him.
this green green boy.
the German bully from
my class,
yes I see
on the bank his
mother crying,
our German Lady Mary
who's embraced her
baby Christ,
screaming
in my ears
infecting me, and
I, unexpectedly, cry too.
why did I echo his mother?
my mouth made loud
sounds.

A DARK GREEN
DEATH.
why did You kill him?
he was a bully, he was my bully.

IX

it's your mistake
foolish Death.
he wasn't a fascist,
he plainly did not want to
study in school,
his boyish temper
hated it. and he hated
my quiet yielding temper.
his actions were like he said,
you need to be a man
you! crazy Death!
his beating me up was only an
invitation to me to become more of a sport,
to become more of a man.
it's wrong,
Hans needs to live,
hey Hans, get up!

X

remember
a hundred years ago
your German, our Russian,
Catherine the Great
saddled
you up, Hans the bully,
to sit on a Volga tractor,
a harvester
to teach us Russians
how to grow bread.
hey Hans, wake up!
we'll wash away
your scary dark dirty green
webbing.
hey Hans,
I hate my textbooks,
my "excellent" marks, my
self-discipline.
I'll join you and all your
bullies.
Hans,
dear bully, come
to me,
please.

RAG DOLL

RAG DOLL

no, he did not look lean skinny
or hungry but he
stared at my spoon,
my porridge,
which I'd warmed up
on a hot spiral plate for my
after-school snack in our
kitchen-anteroom

who?
a captured German solder
in Kazakhstan
(it was the last days of WWII)

I saw lots of them, those German
prisoners, lots
walking idly along the dusty streets of our
settlement.
we schoolboys ran behind them
crying "Fritz Fritz! hey, Fri–i–itz!
now you're here. fascists. Fritz."

our door was open
because my father had come home for lunch:
he was with us,
he had a permit from his work camp,

he could live with his family
for that month

okay

this German guy
pushed open an unlocked door by chance
and walked freely down the street
and somehow entered where we were.
he was tall,
as I remember, in his loose-fitting
German khaki uniform,
and I was a boy,
8? or 9? maybe.
I was not afraid, seeing him,
my father was watching

I stood
so close to the unbidden guest,
he was so young,
I was surprised to see him up close.
I looked at him as if he were a model
I'd already begun painting
I remember his smooth almost fey face
his pale skin, the blush on his puffy
cheeks,
the soft downy hair that clung to his chin,
a giant but a boy.
I almost liked him

why is he a fascist? I wondered
for that moment,
hilarious,
I looked at him with real curiosity,
he examined me, too

and I even smiled
as I remember, and for an instant
I imagined:
this giant-boy, this Fritz,
would run along with us,
leading us,
imitating his
German accent: Fritz Fritz Fritz.
I was always a foolish dreamer

the soldier stepped ahead

he saw something new
he saw a sizzling pan on a scorching plate.
I stood between him and the
inviting smell of food.
his round greedy eyes x-rayed
an aluminum pan.
his look changed abruptly,
and frightened, I stepped back,
stepped back into the doorway

and unexpectedly

I was shoved out by my father's
hand!
(it's time to tell,
he'd been a wrestler before the war,
champion of his Leningrad
sport club
[alas, I didn't inherit this
talent])

I was
dumbstruck, numb, rigid.
in a second (as I remember)
a hapless German boy was lying on the
wood floor,
the German boy,
a rag doll being beaten
by my father

a German boy's (soldier's) face
turned from
pale European to
raw scarlet,
pouring

BLOOOOOOOD!

a pulsing flood from
his wrecked nose
spurting in all directions: hair,

ears, neck,
onto
the German khaki,
producing a picturesque
burnt-umber green military
aesthetic installation
on the floor

this trembling bloody khaki sack
was lifted by my father, head-up
and
he was thrown out
through the open door

I saw
my father, hands trembling,
staring at his fists. he did not look
at me
and I did not expect
an explanation,
it was like
furtively watching a movie for
adults

violence lived in his brain.
he'd had a hard life in exile, he was
such a man:
he'd maintained a faith and loyalty to his land
and to himself and yet, having been a political prisoner,

he couldn't even fight in the Great
Patriotic War on a real front against
real fascists.
he was suspected of being
on Hitler's side.
officially he was an enemy

how did people live with this
inside their homes, their hearts?

MAN LI

MAN LI

*Give evil nothing to oppose
and it will disappear by itself.*
—Tao Te Ching

I

Behind the wall is a laundry.
Man Li is working there, he is Chinese.
He is condemned like all my family
To live in Kazakhstan.

He is my good friend. I like him very much,
With all his characteristics:
His toothless funny smile,
His seemingly eyeless agile face,

His peculiar chirping bird speech
(He doesn't speak Russian).
I miss him during school hours.
I am a schoolboy, 9 or 10 or 11.

Shucking my school bag at home I
Run toward his semi-dark realm and
Without a "Hi! Good day!" but just a nod.
This is our language.

For me
He is a mime.

(In a colonial club I saw such body language
In a German movie, a relic from WWII)
The scenery all around playing on my teenage
Imagination as a future artist:
A huge cast-iron tub filled with boiling water

Reminds me of a monumental living sculpture
Hissing loudly in a foggy room
(Today it would be called a functional installation),
And as for the surrounding stage,

Rain dropping from the ceiling,
Puddles on an earthen floor.
I like Man Li's solid wooden table, our desk, our
School board.

The space of our international communication!
A stack of packed washed cloths
A big hot iron, red inside.

II

"Let's go?" I ask as a command. Man Li knows
What this means. He smiles,
Pouring into the
Aluminum mug a dark liquid smelling of grass

Called Chinese tea
And he stirs in saccharin with an aluminum
Spoon.
I nod impatiently. "It's time!"
And he puts a piece of rope on the table:
Clapping his chest, pointing to mine.
Oh so easy, a snaky rope is the real
Border between me, the Soviet Union,

And him,
China.
And he howls, Uh-h-h! Uh-h-h, the sound
Of a building storm.

He waves his hands over the table,
Higher higher,
Higher than his head,
Such a thunderstorm above the sea.

I am shivering from cold and water.
"Which sea? The Yellow Sea?

Or the Sea of Okhotsk?"
I help him with the geography.

Man Li grabs hold of my teaspoon,
His hand has become his boat, as a billowing
Wave tosses Man Li's boat far far
From his home in China.

III

Yes. He is a fisherman.
He is alone in his small boat under torn sails
Surrounded by storms.
He suddenly catches a fly and deadens
It in his closed fist
And puts it on a spoon
As a boat—Man Li is a dead fly.
The fly falls into the stormy abuse, on to the table.

I look at the fly and at Li with hope:
Don't drown please, friend Man Li,
Oh,
A Chinese fisherman in a boat

Again.
The fly lies at rest on the boat's bottom,
The waves are subsiding,
The boat-spoon rides evenly on the still waves

Man Li is happy.
He sees the shore on the horizon.
Alas, it's not his China.
He looks at the sky and knows where he

Needs to sail.
Man Li is alarmed.
He takes a soup ladle from the stove.

He puts it near the sailing spoon and

On the table with his finger he draws
The Star.
I know it, it is the Soviet symbol.
For me, he points to his forehead,

A Soviet hat with a star,
My teaspoon is inside a soup
Ladle, aluminum like a real military ship.
A Chinese fisherman is captured,

Man Li cries sorrowfully,
Wipes his closed eyes,
"I am not a spy! I am a peaceful fisherman."
He beats his old skinny chest with his fist,

Many many stars appear on the table,
Man Li draws and draws and draws,
"Stop," I hear my boyish voice
Slanted by his grief.

IV

Man Li hides behind the door and then, once more,
He comes to our room.
In his own documentary silent film he enters Kazakhstan.

His quiet somber smile,
"Welcome, Man Li!" I tell him warmly,
"Now we are together. We are friends.
You lost your children,

Now I am your son.
Man Li! My tea is cold, please pour me a hot tea,
And yourself, a tea sweetened with saccharine."

EPILOGUE

Once I rushed into
Man Li's laundry: "Hey, Man Li! Hey!
If you're Man Li, you are not
A fisherman. Do not lie to me.
I read in a history of China in
My school library
You are really Li, but also Zicheng, born Li Hongji,
Don't deny it.
It was the 17th century and I saw your
Engraved portrait.
You are the living image of this guy,
The seemingly eyeless face
And the toothless smile.
You disappeared from Beijing
Mysteriously, but now you are here.
I found you, Man Li.
You were a Chinese rebel leader,
You overthrew the Ming Dynasty
And became the King of your own dynasty
And as King you needed to know many languages.
Do not pretend you don't know Russian.
Initially you were a shepherd,
A cavalry man and a good archer.
You were a Flying Fox on Snowy Mountain,
Man Li, you are the King
But

Your power didn't last long,you were exiled to
Us.
Man Li, we're friends. I'll try to help you
If you don't lie
You were brought here by our Red Star hats.
I read and now know. Man Li, listen.
You were a rebel against feudalism,
Your revolutionary slogans sounded above the
Yellow River. It's like you were a
Supporter of our Russian revolution.
Man Li. Man Li. Man Li.
And now we can reveal the unfairness of your situation
And you will go home, my fool, Man Li, the King.
I have my inkpot here.
Man Li, don't smile like you do not know,
Please work with me,
We'll sit and write a strong detailed appeal
To our fair Soviet leader."
My still unbroken soprano was accompanied
By the steaming noisy boiling water
Of Man Li's laundry.

CHECHEN
RHAPSODY

CHECHEN RHAPSODY

LOUSY CLUB

The Stalinist regime accused the Chechens of massive collaboration with the German invaders during WWII, and then deported them en masse to Kazakhstan in February of 1944.

Far from the blasting epicentre to
Kazakhstan
In time of War,
The serene but bitingly cold continental
Winter,
The fire of the sun aflame
In a sky of sheer light,
The pinching frost.

I am a boy beginning school,
Surviving here with my exiled family.
I am not frozen, I'm
Warmed by my big fur hat,
My high felt boots creak
On the sparkling blinding snow.

What happened during the night?
Above the snowy square between the
Barracks loud guttural voices hang,
Children weeping.

I see a sombre crowd.
A fire burns unseen, the sun
Behind a tall dark curtain.
All kinds of large birds
Take off
And land on the white snow in
Our settlement.
I notice all of them are
Women women women.
And small children bundled in bulky
Clothes to keep warm.
No men.
All are drowned in snowdrifts.
Some of the women shift
On their haunches,
A light steam rises from their ritual
Blazing braziers.

Above a moving crowd
I see

Rising motionless creatures.
Are they men? That's my guess,
Yes,
Old old men, crowned by tall black
Sheepskin hats,
Silhouetted Easter Island sculptures,
Mountain gods mounting the snow.
I get closer,

Some of them, already frozen, are dead,
Surrounded by
Wailing women.

My child's consciousness
Cannot comprehend…

At home my mother answers me:

"They are repatriated from the
Caucasus Mountains, they are Chechens.
They joined up with German troops
To fight for their freedom against Russia
So
Their families are here, no men, and
They hide in the mountains or are in jail.
The oldest is over a hundred.
By the way, go to the bookshelf.
It seems to me
In Tolstoy we have Hadji Murad,
A Chechen hero from the past."

My parents do not tell me that we are
Exiled like these Chechens,
My parents, so far as I know, came
to Kazakhstan
From Leningrad to work.
They were in
The forefront of a workers call.

In a couple of days
The crowd melted away.
They were settled in our spacious barn
Where I watched captured
German
War movies.

The Chechens didn't
Settle in the housing barracks
Until the spring
And our social club was closed down for a long
Time
For sanitary reasons:
The overcrowded Chechens
Bred and fed infected
Vermin on their
Unwashed bodies.

Later, optimistic local people
Named the barn the "Lousy Club."
It was a joke:
"At our Lousy Club, on its silver screen,
The German movie *Diva*—
Marika Rekk
Has the itch in her long eugenic legs,
The rhythm
Of her sparkling dance."

Recently I read on the Internet that
Ms. Rekk,
The Girl of Hitler's Dreams,
Was not an ideal Aryan,
She was (such catastrophe)
A Hungarian,
And by the way, her father was
An architect.
But the Führer,
If he'd been wise like our Stalin, he
Could have repatriated the
German cinematic goddess to our
Settlement along with the Chechens.

Who is this Marika Rekk?
My boyhood brain meditates...
She is only a pretty dancing girl
For I have read about Hadji Murad
In a book from our bookshelf
And dreamed
Of seeing our Lousy Club
Movie of the breathtaking
Caucasus Mountains
With their
Galloping horseman Hadji Murad as a
Red Army commander.

I kept my brave vision to myself,
Didn't even share it with my parents.

HADJI MURAD

*In 1851 the young count Leo Tolstoy was sent to the
Caucasus to help defeat the Chechens. During this war a
chieftain, Hadji Murad, broke with the Chechen leader
and fled to the Russians for safety. Months later, while
attempting to rescue his family, Hadji Murad was pursued
by those he had betrayed and, after fighting the most heroic
battle of his life, was killed. The story was prefaced by a
description of a crushed, but still living thistle in a field—
a symbol of the strong, brave, and manly character of
the Highlander, Hadji Murad.*

"I am returning home by the field,"
Leo Tolstoy begins his tale.

"It's midsummer and it is time to reap the rye…"
I shall continue the story in my own words:

Tolstoy's attention is attracted to the
Delightful variety of field wild flowers,

Red white bright-blue lilac
Growing among green grasses,

So multi-coloured and so gentle.
Tolstoy gathers a large nosegay

Before he goes home
But he also notices a big thistle in full bloom.

It has a pleasant crimson flower.
He tries bypassing the prickly dragon

But this bouquet lover is seized by
An idea—

Put the bright red flower
In his ikebana.

Even with his handkerchief
He cannot control the plant.

But he is stubborn,
He breaks the hard stem's fibres

One by one.
Still, the obstinate flower wins.

It is not fresh
And beautiful like it was but still red

As it had been
Apart from the bouquet:

"Sorry for the vanity inherent in destroying
A moment in nature."

Tolstoy meditates, he lets us track his sorrow:
What is man? This wild rude creature,

No mercy. No compassion. No pity.
No forbearance.

VANESSA'S MONOLOGUE

*The English film star and famous theatre actress, Vanessa
Redgrave, stepped in to help in the release of fellow actor,
Akhmed Zakayev, accused of being a Chechen rebel envoy,
accused by the Russian authority of mass murder. He is
seeking political asylum in the UK. Redgrave's daughter,
Natasha Richardson, died in New York in 2009 after she
fell while skiing in Quebec.*

Oh Akhie, dear! Listen.
Where are you? Downstairs
In the living room?
I'll go down

From my bedroom,
Down the spiral staircase.
Good morning.
Couldn't sleep last night,
I could hardly sleep night after night
Because of our political discussions about the
Chechen question.
But finally I fell asleep in the early morning.
I woke up to
The sun at play in the glazed attic—
O Akhie, dear, I have news
I need to tell you,
It is serious.

I think that any citizen can understand that
You must raise your voice.

My world, oh Akhie,
Is this a world only of opponents?
As your world is full of enemies?
Please, dear, do not talk on your cell,
Tell them you need to rest in the morning.
Please, Mary, bring me strong black coffee.
Oh Akhie!

I think that any citizen can understand that
You must raise your voice.

I had an ominous dream,
I am still shivering.
I had a long discussion with Natasha,
My loving daughter who left suddenly,
I'm scared.
I love her very much.
She told me that for the sake
Of her short life I need to keep this in mind—
I am an actress.
"Do not forget it," she said.
"What you're doing today is dangerous,
Like my skiing.
My Quebec, my damned ski trip."
But I said to my poor daughter:

I think that any citizen can understand that
You must raise your voice.

And she said,
"It's not for you. Forget your past."
She said,
"Your Palestinian dance,
A Kalashnikov in your artistic hands
YouTubed to the curious world of YouTube-users
Of the '80s!"
She said,
"Forget your Oscar speech with your words about the
'Zionist hoodlums.'
Stop trying to astonish the whole world."
She said,
"Oh, it was fancy in the '60s
With the flower child revolution,
Along with Beatlemania."
Oh my poor daughter.
She cannot understand how I think:

I think that any citizen can understand that
You must raise your voice.

Oh please, turn off your cell, Akhmet.
"Catch, Mum, running away with time.
You are not a marching girl,"
She said.
Oh my poor daughter.

"But you are still Queen Gertrude.
Too bad I wasn't
Born Ophelia, as my father said to me
Now I am absent, alas, all is not within my control.
You have your own Hamlet.
Your Chechen friend is not a galloping
Highlander,
Not Hadji Murad by Leo Tolstoy.
He is an actor. It's his profession.
You are lucky, Mum."
She embraced my shoulders as I shook—
Oh my poor daughter. But,

I think that any citizen can understand that
You must raise your voice.

"You adopted him
As a son.
And as a mother you can stop him.
Oh yes.
Persuade him to work for the theatre.
He was a Chechen Hamlet.
Not the political stage, but
As an envoy.
To the real stage, the theatre!
Not to play in the Moscow musical *Nord-West*,
Aka like Russians say, a bandit leader.
Oh Mum.
Chechnya was always Russian."

Her insistence irritates me.
Oh my poor daughter! But,

I think that any citizen can understand that
You must raise your voice.

"Instead of investing in
The blood of war or
Crazy money for Akhmed's bail,
Invest in the Chechen Theatre in Groznyy
On behalf of your restless theatrical soul.
For his—your Chechen son, your friend—the theatre's
Renovation.
For the world's cultural resonance.
For all of us to enjoy.
For our family—
We always were a kind of 'arts' royalty."
You are so sentimental, I thought.
Oh my poor daughter. But,

I think that any citizen can understand that
You must raise your voice.

She did not hear me. Oh my daughter...
"You can invite the Royal Haymarket,"
She said,
"To produce the Groznyy international premier.
To get the Olivier Award
For your Akhmet Hamlet,

The man of soft features,
A politician by mistake."
I saw tears in her eyes.
"It's time to end.—Oh Mum.
As a farewell, sing to me again
My 'Edelweiss.'"
You know, Akhmet,
I began to sing this song
Many years ago:

> *Edelweiss edelweiss*
> *Every morning you greet me*
> *Small and white*
> *Clean and bright…*

Smiling, she disappeared.
Oh my poor daughter.
What do you think, Akhie? What do I think?
You know:

> *I think that any citizen can understand that*
> *You must raise your voice.*

Mary, please, no cream in my coffee.
I take skimmed milk but warm it up, please.
Is my car ready for the day?
Thank you, one cup's enough.

I think that any citizen can understand that
You must raise your voice.

Akhmed, you will continue to talk on the phone
In the car, and oh Akhie,

I almost forgot.
You are busy but you
Need to drop me off at my film set
To see my Nathaniel—
Who is Nathaniel, you ask again.
I told you so many times.
Ralph Fiennes.
He needs you, wants to ask you, he has one
Psychological theatrical request:
What Does He Feel? Coriolanus.
Not in Shakespeare's drama, but
Today, when friends
Betray him. Be ready to be interviewed,
Not at the trial, but for art, or for real life.
What do you say? What?
What do I think about? A-a-h!
You know my answer:

I think that any citizen can understand that
You must raise your voice.

COSSACK LULLABY

Historically, for centuries, the small Chechen nation has engaged in an almost constant battle for independence. These militant highlanders were a great danger to their Slavic neighbours, even the brave Cossacks, who settled there in the sixteenth century to guard the Russian frontier. The "vicious Chechen" is a justifiably notorious phrase to Russian ears. We hear it in a poem, "Cossack Lullaby," by Mikhail Lermontov, who was exiled to the Caucasian front to fight with the mountain rebels in the early nineteenth century. In this poem, in my translation, as a Cossack mother lulls her child, she conjures up a knife-wielding Chechen as a bogeyman:

Sleep, my little one, my baby,
Lullaby and goodnight,
The clear sky above your cradle
In the bright moon's light.
Fairy tales rock you gently
As my song flies on high.
Close your eyes and sleep, ever sweetly,

Lullaby and goodnight.

Through the rocks the river Terek
Drives its troubled stream,
The evil Chechen crawls,
His sharp blade gleams.

Your father is a warrior,
He has simply to die
As guardian of your dreams, ever dreaming,

Lullaby and goodnight.

Time flows by fields of battle,
Battle overtakes our land.
You, horseman with a rifle,
Ride along the strand.
Your embroidered saddle flashes,
Galloping hooves fly.
Sleep soundly, my future soldier, soundly sleep,

Lullaby and goodnight.

You will grow to be a warrior
With a Cossack soul.
I will see you off to battle
As you follow the call of the roll.
I'll hide my tears of sorrow,
Swallowing my sigh.
Sleep, my angel, sleep sweetly, ever sweetly,

Lullaby and goodbye.

TOLSTOY IS THE GREATEST NOVELIST

Tolstoy is the greatest novelist.
— VIRGINIA WOOLF

"I am returning home by the field.
 It's midsummer and it is time

To reap the rye."
This is how his classic story begins,

The thistle, fighting for its life,
Is an overture to Tolstoy's tale of

A brave Caucasian hero,
Hadji Murad,

Martyr to a sacred fight for Freedom
Two hundred years ago.

For Murad, independence was a solemn
Flag atop a high mountain!

And for all
For what was—

His life, his faithfulness to the folk,
His honest military diplomacy—

His death after the thistle's long heroic
Resistance.

Hadji Murad rides to his mountain
Village, Clear transparent air,

A bright sunny sky,
A virgin stillness,

The rhythmic clatter of hooves
Accompanies the horseman,

And from time to time loose stones
Fall

Producing a light clattering
Down the slopes—

Be watchful as you ride
Through

The Caucasus Mountains,
Hadji Murad thinks, smiling...

....

"But suddenly he shuddered.
Like a scythed thistle he fell full length

On his face
And moved no more.

He did not move but could still feel.
The first to reach him

Put a boot on his body's back, and took
Two strokes to hack off his head

And roll it carefully away
So as not to get blood

On the leather of his boot as
Blood gushed through the grass,

Scarlet from the neck arteries,
Black from the head…

Nightingales again burst
Into song…

This was the crushed thistle in the
Ploughed field…"

AUTHOR'S NOTES

Seven Lives consists of "visuals" that recall Russian life under the former "scarlet" Soviet flag. The bright red colour has faded with historical re-examination of the communist regime, now that the blood has dried. Our memories tend to find a poetic lens for our past experiences, especially those of our childhood and youth.

Overture. The "Song of the Volga Boatmen" ("Yo, Heave Ho!") is a genuine shanty song sung by burlaks, or barge-haulers, on the Volga River. The song inspired Ilya Repin's famous painting, *Barge Haulers on the Volga*, which depicts burlaks in Tsarist Russia. The song was popularized by the famous Russian singer, Feodor Chaliapin, and has been a favourite concert piece of bass singers ever since. Glenn Miller's rather awful syncopated arrangement took the song to #1 in the US charts in 1941.

"To Aunt Shura." This poem is about a real meeting in Moscow with my 93-year-old aunt in the summer of 2011. I wanted to give the reader a picture of a typical Russian woman who had the mentality of the WWII period. She was the former wife of a military man and had devoted her life to him. "Yo, heave ho!" is a refrain that helped Aunt Shura survive a hard life.

"Leningrad." The poem begins with Stalinist repression, the murder of the Leningrad Communist leader Sergei Kirov in 1934, and the introduction of draconian laws enacted to punish "political crimes." Stalin's paranoiac fear of thinking people paved the way for the Great Terror of the '30s. My parents – one exiled to the Gulag and other banished to Kazakhstan – were among the victims of this Terror.

"A Cow Named Beauty." My poetic memory of a kind member of our family during a time of severe exile.

"Green Drowning." My childhood memory of a conflict with a classmate, a boy-bully of Volga-German background, repatriated with his mother to Kazakhstan during WWII. In the eighteenth century, Catherine the Great had invited people from Germany to develop Russian agriculture. The Empress could not have foreseen the future that lay ahead for them.

"Rag Doll." A poem about my boyish attitude to captive military Germans after WWII.

"Man Li." A poem about a Chinese fisherman. While at sea, a storm blew his ship into Russian waters. He was exiled to Kazakhstan as a spy. Man Li suffered the same emotional violence as many Russians of that time.

"Chechen Rhapsody." An appeal for a balanced and peaceful approach to the old conflict in the Northern Caucasian region of Russia, which has in recent years escalated into an endless guerilla war.

ACKNOWLEDGEMENTS

Many thanks to the editor-in-chief of Exile Editions, Barry Callaghan, for his creative involvement in these stories of my Russian life during the Soviet regime, for his vibrant attitude toward the culture and the history of my home country, which he has visited on several occasions. I would like to thank the publisher of Exile Editions, Michael Callaghan, for his intensive work in the publishing process of my books. I would like to thank poet Jay MillAr, who was one of the first readers of my manuscript. A big thank you to Ewan Whyte, for his willingness to discuss my poetry and for his preface to *Seven Lives*. My thanks to artist Deborah Barnett who provided the illustrations that appear in the book.

Vladimir Azarov is an architect and poet,
formerly from Moscow, who lives in Toronto.
He has published *Dinner With Catherine the Great,*
Territories, Mongolian Études, Seven Lives,
Broken Pastries, Night Out, Imitation,
Strong Words: Pushkin, Akhmatova, Voznesensky
a Russian and English edition (translated with Barry Callaghan),
Of Life and Other Small Sacrifices,
The Kiss from Mary Pickford: Cinematic Poems,
and *Voices in Dialogue: Dramatic Poems.*

Artsit Deborah Barnett produces illustrations for poetry, small and large-scale paintings, and 3Dimensional multi media works. She is also the Creative Director of the someone.ca design and letterpress studio in Toronto.